TEXAS TEST PREP

Practice Test Book

STAAR Math

Grade 4

ISBN 978-1463572686

CONTENTS

INTRODUCTION

For Parents, Teachers, and Tutors

About the Book

This test book contains three complete STAAR math grade 4 tests. The tests are just like the STAAR tests given by the state. Each test contains 42 questions, which is the same as the state test. Each test also has the same question types and styles, and tests the same skills.

If the student can master the STAAR mathematics tests in this book, they will be prepared and ready to master the STAAR state tests.

Taking the Test

Each test contains 42 multiple choice questions. Students can answer the questions by filling in the circle of their answer choice in the test booklet. Students can also answer the questions by filling in the circles on the answer sheet in the back of the book.

Score Tracker

After marking each test, record the score in the Score Tracker at the end of the book to see the student's improvement as they gain experience, knowledge, and confidence.

STAAR Math Skills

The STAAR test given by the state of Texas tests a specific set of skills and knowledge. The skills and knowledge tested are described in the TEKS Student Expectations. These expectations list all the skills and knowledge that students are expected to have and are divided into six broad objectives. If a student has all the skills listed in the TEKS, they will master the STAAR test.

The answer key for each test lists the objective and the student expectation for each question. Use the answer key and the objective list to determine the areas of strength and the areas of weakness. Then target revision and instruction accordingly. Use the student expectations to identify the specific skills and knowledge that the student is lacking. Then target revision and instruction accordingly.

The list of objectives and student expectations are included in the back of the book.

STAAR Math Quiz Book

For additional revision and practice, get the Texas Test Prep Student Quiz Book. It contains one quiz for every skill tested on the STAAR test, and allows students to focus on each TEKS Student Expectation individually.

It is the perfect way to target gaps in knowledge and focus on improving a student's areas of weakness.

STAAR MATH

GRADE 4

TEST 1

Instructions

The test contains 42 multiple-choice questions. Read each question carefully. Then select the best answer. Fill in the circle for the correct answer.

You can use the mathematic chart on the next page to help you with some of the questions.

MATHEMATICS CHART

You may use this chart to help you answer questions in the test.

LENGTH

Metric
1 meter = 100 centimeters
1 centimeter = 10 millimeters

Customary
1 yard = 3 feet
1 foot = 12 inches

CAPACITY AND VOLUME

Metric
1 liter = 1000 milliliters

Customary
1 gallon = 4 quarts
1 gallon = 128 fluid ounces
1 quart = 2 pints
1 pint = 2 cups
1 cup = 8 fluid ounces

MASS AND WEIGHT

Metric
1 kilogram = 1000 grams
1 gram = 1000 milligrams

Customary
1 ton = 2000 pounds
1 pound = 16 ounces

TIME

Metric
1 year = 365 days
1 year = 12 months
1 year = 52 weeks

Customary
1 week = 7 days
1 day = 24 hours
1 hour = 60 minutes

1   The table below shows the total number of pieces of bread Aaron used to make peanut butter and jelly sandwiches.

Number of Sandwiches	Number of Pieces of Bread
2	6
4	8
8	24

Which of the following describes the relationship in the table?

   Ⓐ   Number of sandwiches × 2 = number of pieces of bread

   Ⓑ   Number of sandwiches × 3 = number of pieces of bread

   Ⓒ   Number of sandwiches × 6 = number of pieces of bread

   Ⓓ   Number of sandwiches × 8 = number of pieces of bread

2   A jug of milk contains 4 pints of milk. Michael pours 1 cup of milk from the jug. How much milk is left in the jug?

    Ⓐ   3 cups

    Ⓑ   6 cups

    Ⓒ   7 cups

    Ⓓ   8 cups

3   Donna bought a lollipop for 60 cents and a candy for 15 cents. How much change would Donna receive from $1?

    Ⓐ   15 cents

    Ⓑ   25 cents

    Ⓒ   35 cents

    Ⓓ   75 cents

4   Victor rode 3 kilometers to his friend's house. How many meters did Victor ride?

Ⓐ   30 meters

Ⓑ   300 meters

Ⓒ   3,000 meters

Ⓓ   30,000 meters

5   The thermometers below show the air temperature at 10 a.m. and 2 p.m. one day.

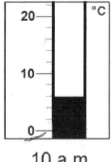
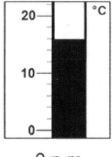

10 a.m.   2 p.m.

How much did the temperature rise by from 10 a.m. to 2 p.m.?

Ⓐ   5°C

Ⓑ   6°C

Ⓒ   10°C

Ⓓ   16°C

6 Mario bought a packet of 8 crayons. How can he find how many crayons he would have if he bought 4 packets of crayons?

    Ⓐ   Divide 8 by 4

    Ⓑ   Add 4 to 8

    Ⓒ   Subtract 4 from 8

    Ⓓ   Multiply 8 by 4

7   The table below shows the cost of food at a diner.

Drinks		Meals	
Small milkshake	$1.80	Plain hamburger	$3.50
Large milkshake	$2.00	Chicken burger	$4.20
Small soda	$1.10	Hotdog	$2.50
Large soda	$1.50	Meatball sub	$3.10
Fruit juice	$1.90	Quiche	$2.10

Lisa bought 2 items and spent exactly $4.00. Which two items could Lisa have bought?

Ⓐ   Meatball sub and a fruit juice

Ⓑ   Plain hamburger and a large soda

Ⓒ   Large soda and a hotdog

Ⓓ   Quiche and a small milkshake

8 Jayden wants to find the length of a paperclip. Which unit would Jayden be best to use?

(A) Millimeters

(B) Milligrams

(C) Grams

(D) Kilometers

9 The table below shows the entry cost for a museum.

Adult	$10 per person
Child	$6 per person
Family (2 adults and 2 children)	$30 per family

How much would it cost for 1 adult and 2 children to go to the museum?

Ⓐ $22

Ⓑ $26

Ⓒ $30

Ⓓ $32

10 George wrote the set of expressions below.

$$6 + 4 \qquad 5 \times 2 \qquad 5 + 5 \qquad 14 - 4$$

Which expression could be added to the set?

Ⓐ $6 - 4$

Ⓑ $5 + 6$

Ⓒ 10×2

Ⓓ $20 \div 2$

11 Mrs. Morgan is choosing the design of a business card. The picture below shows the patterns and the colors available.

| Plain |
| Stars |
| Stripes |

Pink	Green
Blue	Red
Yellow	Gray

How many combinations of 1 pattern and 1 color are possible?

Ⓐ   9

Ⓑ   12

Ⓒ   18

Ⓓ   36

12 Which of the following describes the rule for this pattern?

1, 3, 6, 8, 11, 13, 16

Ⓐ   Add 2, add 3

Ⓑ   Add 2, multiply by 2

Ⓒ   Multiply by 3, multiply by 2

Ⓓ   Multiply by 3, add 3

13   David filled the bucket below with water.

About how much water would it take to fill the bucket?

Ⓐ   5 milliliters

Ⓑ   5 pints

Ⓒ   5 liters

Ⓓ   5 quarts

14   Which point on the number line represents 2.5?

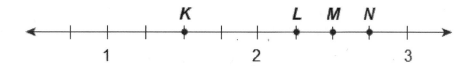

Ⓐ   Point *K*

Ⓑ   Point *L*

Ⓒ   Point *M*

Ⓓ   Point *N*

15   Which of the following diagrams shows a translation?

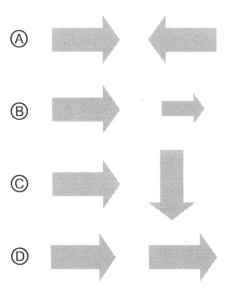

16   Maria is reading a book with 286 pages. She has read 38 pages. Which is the best estimate of how many pages Maria has left to read?

Ⓐ   240

Ⓑ   250

Ⓒ   260

Ⓓ   270

17 A pizza can be cut into 8 slices. Lee ordered 7 pizzas for a party. How many slices of pizza did Lee order?

Ⓐ   42

Ⓑ   48

Ⓒ   56

Ⓓ   64

18 The table below shows the population of 3 towns.

Town	Population
Franklin	18,725
Torine	24,214
Maxville	16,722

Which number sentence shows the best way to estimate how much greater the population of Torine is than Franklin?

Ⓐ   24,000 – 16,000 = 8,000

Ⓑ   24,000 – 17,000 = 7,000

Ⓒ   24,000 – 18,000 = 6,000

Ⓓ   24,000 – 19,000 = 5,000

19 Erin is sorting her dimes into piles. She puts the dimes in piles of 5. She has a total of 65 dimes.

How many piles of dimes would Erin have?

Ⓐ   11

Ⓑ   12

Ⓒ   13

Ⓓ   15

20 A box of beads contains 100 beads. Chang buys 5 boxes of beads. How many beads did Chang buy?

Ⓐ   105

Ⓑ   500

Ⓒ   150

Ⓓ   5,000

21 A car traveled 52 miles in 1 hour. About how long would it take the car to travel 265 miles?

Ⓐ   5 hours

Ⓑ   4 hours

Ⓒ   3 hours

Ⓓ   6 hours

22   Look at the figure below.

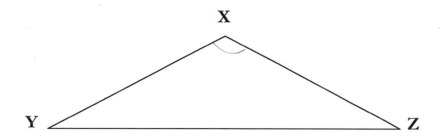

Which angles appear to be obtuse?

Ⓐ   Angle X only

Ⓑ   Angle Y only

Ⓒ   Angle X and angle Z

Ⓓ   Angle Y and angle Z

23   Look at the figure below.

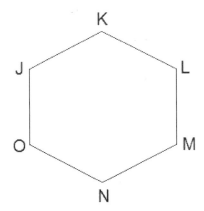

How many pairs of parallel sides does the figure appear to have?

Ⓐ   0

Ⓑ   1

Ⓒ   2

Ⓓ   3

24 Which number sentence is in the same fact family as 8 × 5 = 40?

    Ⓐ   40 ÷ 5 = 8

    Ⓑ   8 × 8 = 64

    Ⓒ   40 + 5 = 45

    Ⓓ   5 × 40 = 200

25 How many vertices does the square pyramid shown below have?

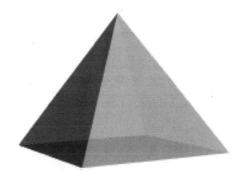

    Ⓐ   4

    Ⓑ   5

    Ⓒ   6

    Ⓓ   8

26 Which single transformation could have changed Figure F to Figure G?

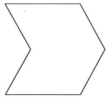

Figure F   Figure G

Ⓐ   Rotation

Ⓑ   Reflection

Ⓒ   Translation

Ⓓ   Not here

27   Which letter has 2 lines of symmetry?

Ⓐ   Z

Ⓑ   Y

Ⓒ   X

Ⓓ   W

28 The model below was made with 1-unit cubes.

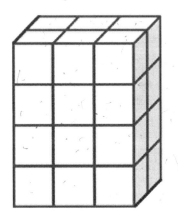

What is the volume of the model?

Ⓐ 16 cubic units

Ⓑ 24 cubic units

Ⓒ 26 cubic units

Ⓓ 48 cubic units

29   How many lines of symmetry does the shape below have?

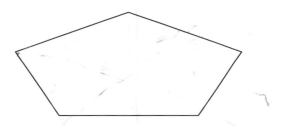

Ⓐ   0

Ⓑ   1

Ⓒ   2

Ⓓ   5

30 The model below was made with 1-inch cubes.

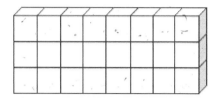

What is the volume of the model?

Ⓐ   22 cubic inches

Ⓑ   24 cubic inches

Ⓒ   64 cubic inches

Ⓓ   72 cubic inches

31   The graph below shows the number of points 6 players
scored in a basketball game.

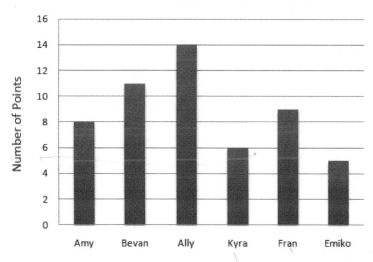

How many points did Kyra and Fran score together?

(A)   6

(B)   9

(C)   15

(D)   16

32 Dora bought 4 packets of pens. There were 8 pens in each packet. Which number sentence can be used to find the total number of pens?

Ⓐ $8 + 4 = \square$

Ⓑ $8 \div 8 = \square$

Ⓒ $8 \times 4 = \square$

Ⓓ $8 - 4 = \square$

33 Joel bought a notepad for $1.25 and a pen for $1.65. How much money did Joel spend in all?

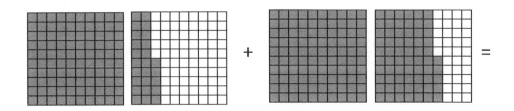

Ⓐ $2.70

Ⓑ $2.80

Ⓒ $2.90

Ⓓ $3.00

34   There are 40,260 people watching a baseball game. Which of these is another way to write 40,260?

Ⓐ   4 + 2 + 6

Ⓑ   40 + 2 + 60

Ⓒ   40,000 + 200 + 6

Ⓓ   40,000 + 200 + 60

35   The model below is shaded to show $2\frac{4}{10}$.

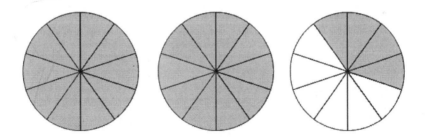

Which decimal does the model represent?

Ⓐ   2.04

Ⓑ   2.4

Ⓒ   0.24

Ⓓ   20.4

36 Which of the following is another way to write the numeral 600,032?

    Ⓐ   Six hundred thousand and thirty-two

    Ⓑ   Six million and thirty-two

    Ⓒ   Six hundred and thirty-two

    Ⓓ   Six thousand and thirty-two

37 Which number sentence represents the array shown below?

    Ⓐ $5 + 3 = 8$

    Ⓑ $5 \times 3 = 15$

    Ⓒ $15 \times 3 = 45$

    Ⓓ $20 - 5 = 15$

38 The table below shows the number of male and female students at Hill Street School.

Gender	Number
Male	2,629
Female	2,518

How many students go to the school in all?

Ⓐ 5,147

Ⓑ 5,137

Ⓒ 4,137

Ⓓ 5,247

39 Mitch ran 2.6 miles on Monday and 1.8 miles on Tuesday. How many miles less did Mitch run on Tuesday?

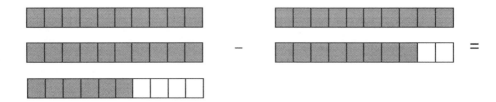

Ⓐ 0.2 miles

Ⓑ 1.2 miles

Ⓒ 1.8 miles

Ⓓ 0.8 miles

40 What is the product of 4 and 12?

Ⓐ 44

Ⓑ 36

Ⓒ 48

Ⓓ 60

41 A pet shop sells fish for $3 each. The pet shop sold 12 fish. What is the total cost of the fish?

(A) $24

(B) $36

(C) $33

(D) $39

42 Which pair of numbers completes the equation below?

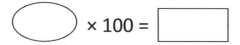

(A) 60 and 6,000

(B) 60 and 60,000

(C) 6 and 60

(D) 6 and 6,000

END OF TEST

STAAR MATH

GRADE 4

TEST 2

Instructions

The test contains 42 multiple-choice questions. Read each question carefully. Then select the best answer. Fill in the circle for the correct answer.

You can use the mathematic chart on the next page to help you with some of the questions.

MATHEMATICS CHART

You may use this chart to help you answer questions in the test.

LENGTH

Metric
1 meter = 100 centimeters
1 centimeter = 10 millimeters

Customary
1 yard = 3 feet
1 foot = 12 inches

CAPACITY AND VOLUME

Metric
1 liter = 1000 milliliters

Customary
1 gallon = 4 quarts
1 gallon = 128 fluid ounces
1 quart = 2 pints
1 pint = 2 cups
1 cup = 8 fluid ounces

MASS AND WEIGHT

Metric
1 kilogram = 1000 grams
1 gram = 1000 milligrams

Customary
1 ton = 2000 pounds
1 pound = 16 ounces

TIME

Metric
1 year = 365 days
1 year = 12 months
1 year = 52 weeks

Customary
1 week = 7 days
1 day = 24 hours
1 hour = 60 minutes

1   What do the shaded models below show?

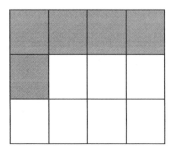 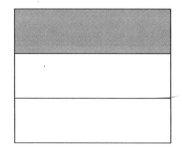

Ⓐ $\dfrac{5}{12} > \dfrac{1}{3}$

Ⓑ $\dfrac{5}{12} = \dfrac{1}{3}$

Ⓒ $\dfrac{5}{12} < \dfrac{4}{12}$

Ⓓ $\dfrac{5}{7} < \dfrac{2}{3}$

2 The model below is shaded to show $\frac{62}{100}$.

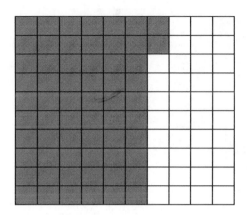

Which decimal does the model represent?

Ⓐ 0.62

Ⓑ 6.2

Ⓒ 60.2

Ⓓ 0.062

3   Which of the following is represented by the grid below?

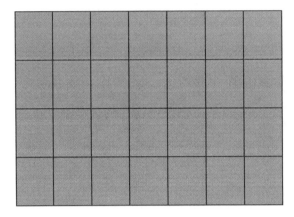

Ⓐ   4 x 4 = 16

Ⓑ   4 x 6 = 24

Ⓒ   4 + 6 = 10

Ⓓ   6 + 6 = 12

4   Each number that was put into the number machine below changed according to a rule.

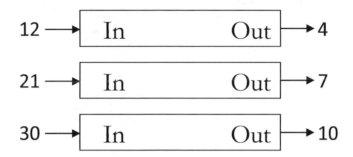

Which equation describes the rule for the number machine?

Ⓐ   Number in × 3 = number out

Ⓑ   Number in + 20 = number out

Ⓒ   Number in ÷ 3 = number out

Ⓓ   Number in − 8 = number out

5   The decimal cards for 0.59 and 0.22 are shown below.

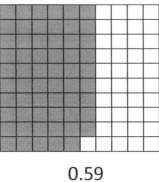   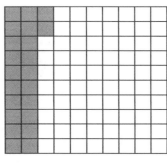

0.59   0.22

What is the difference of 0.59 and 0.22?

Ⓐ   0.39

Ⓑ   0.37

Ⓒ   0.81

Ⓓ   0.83

6 Which fraction does the shaded model represent?

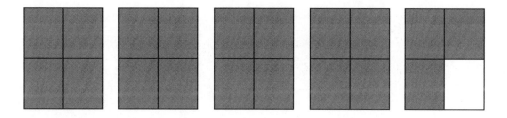

Ⓐ   4¾

Ⓑ   4¼

Ⓒ   5¾

Ⓓ   5¼

7   The shaded model below represents a fraction.

Which model below represents an equivalent fraction?

Ⓐ

Ⓑ

Ⓒ

Ⓓ

8   Which type of angle is shown below?

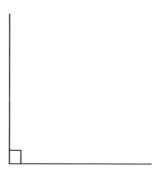

Ⓐ   Acute

Ⓑ   Obtuse

Ⓒ   Straight

Ⓓ   Right

9   Look at the letters below.

F H J L

Which letter has a line of symmetry?

Ⓐ   F

Ⓑ   H

Ⓒ   J

Ⓓ   L

10   Which digit is in the thousands place in the number 6,124,853?

Ⓐ   6

Ⓑ   1

Ⓒ   2

Ⓓ   4

11   Which decimal represents the shaded model below?

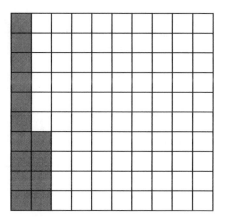

(A)   1.4

(B)   0.014

(C)   0.14

(D)   14.0

12   Which number has a 4 in the ten millions place?

(A)   758,340,386

(B)   845,768,950

(C)   234,082,663

(D)   478,935,159

13 The diagram below shows two sets of black and white stickers.

Which of the following compares the portion of black stickers in each set?

Ⓐ $\frac{8}{9} > \frac{2}{3}$

Ⓑ $\frac{8}{9} < \frac{2}{9}$

Ⓒ $\frac{2}{3} < \frac{1}{3}$

Ⓓ $\frac{1}{9} > \frac{6}{9}$

14 What is the product of 9 and 12?

  Ⓐ 99

  Ⓑ 96

  Ⓒ 120

  Ⓓ 108

15 Ari is putting photos in an album. He can fit 4 photos on each page. How many photos can he fit on 9 pages?

  Ⓐ 27

  Ⓑ 38

  Ⓒ 36

  Ⓓ 24

16   Mrs. Smyth has 82 colored pencils. She wants to divide them evenly between 8 people. How many whole pencils will each person receive?

 Ⓐ 7

 Ⓑ 8

 Ⓒ 10

 Ⓓ 11

17 The grade 4 students at Diane's school are collecting cans for a food drive. The table below shows how many cans each class collected.

Class	Number of Cans
Miss Adams	36
Mr. Walsh	28
Mrs. Naroda	47

Which is the best way to estimate the number of cans collected in all?

Ⓐ   30 + 20 + 40 =

Ⓑ   30 + 30 + 40 =

Ⓒ   40 + 30 + 50 =

Ⓓ   40 + 30 + 40 =

18 Sandy has 129 pennies. Marvin has 185 pennies. How many pennies do Sandy and Marvin have in all?

Ⓐ 314

Ⓑ 315

Ⓒ 214

Ⓓ 215

19   The table below shows the number of students in each grade at the David Hall School.

Grade	Number of Students
3	254
4	235
5	229

How many students are there all together?

Ⓐ   618

Ⓑ   608

Ⓒ   708

Ⓓ   718

20   Which shape could **NOT** have any square faces?

Ⓐ   Cube

Ⓑ   Rectangular prism

Ⓒ   Square pyramid

Ⓓ   Triangular prism

21   Which figure below does NOT have any parallel sides?

Ⓐ

Ⓑ

Ⓒ

Ⓓ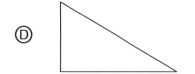

22 Which measurement is the same as 3 feet?

Ⓐ   6 yards

Ⓑ   9 yards

Ⓒ   12 inches

Ⓓ   48 inches

23 The model below was made with 1-cm cubes.

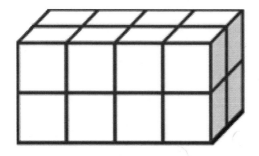

What is the volume of the model?

Ⓐ   8 cubic centimeters

Ⓑ   14 cubic centimeters

Ⓒ   32 cubic centimeters

Ⓓ   16 cubic centimeters

24   The thermometer below shows the temperature at 5 p.m. on Tuesday.

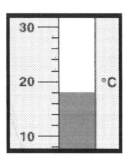

By 10 p.m. on Tuesday, the temperature had dropped by 6°C. What was the temperature at 10 p.m. on Tuesday?

Ⓐ   18°C

Ⓑ   12°C

Ⓒ   14°C

Ⓓ   24°C

25   Ellen selected a number. She followed the set of rules below.

Add 4 to the number.
Divide the number by 2.
Subtract 3 from the number.

The result was 4. What number did Ellen start with?

Ⓐ   6

Ⓑ   1

Ⓒ   10

Ⓓ   18

26 Lloyd bought 4 T-shirts. Each T-shirt cost $7. Which is one way to work out how much change Lloyd would receive from $30?

Ⓐ   Add 4 to 7 and subtract the result from 30

Ⓑ   Add 4 to 7 and add the result to 30

Ⓒ   Multiply 4 by 7 and add the result to 30

Ⓓ   Multiply 4 by 7 and subtract the result from 30

27   Which number sentence represents the array shown below?

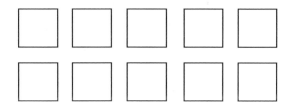

   Ⓐ $5 + 2 = 7$

   Ⓑ $5 \times 5 = 25$

   Ⓒ $5 \times 2 = 10$

   Ⓓ $5 - 2 = 3$

28 Which type of angle best describes angle X?

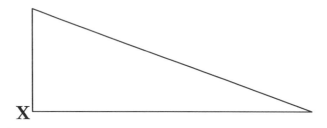

Ⓐ Acute

Ⓑ Obtuse

Ⓒ Straight

Ⓓ Right

29   Look at the line segments shown below.

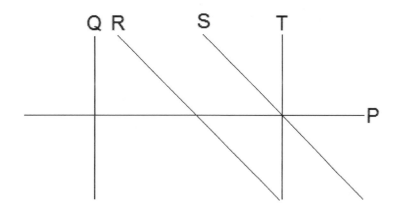

Which two line segments are parallel?

Ⓐ   Line segment P and line segment Q

Ⓑ   Line segment R and line segment S

Ⓒ   Line segment Q and line segment R

Ⓓ   Line segment S and line segment T

30 Mia is setting up tables for a party. Each table can seat 6 people. Mia needs to seat 32 people. How many tables would Mia need?

Ⓐ 3

Ⓑ 4

Ⓒ 5

Ⓓ 6

31 Emma grouped a set of numbers into 2 groups. The groups are shown below.

Group 1	Group 2
14	21
86	79
922	325
388	683

Which number belongs in Group 2?

Ⓐ   18

Ⓑ   630

Ⓒ   864

Ⓓ   247

32 Which number sentence is in the same fact family as $44 \div \square = 11$?

Ⓐ $44 \div 2 = \square$

Ⓑ $\square \times 11 = 44$

Ⓒ $11 \div \square = 44$

Ⓓ $44 \times 11 = \square$

33   Which pair of figures shows a reflection?

34   Which model is shaded to show a fraction equivalent to $\frac{6}{10}$?

35 Which transformation is shown below?

Ⓐ   Rotation

Ⓑ   Reflection

Ⓒ   Translation

Ⓓ   Not here

36 The graph below shows the high temperature in Dallas, Texas for five days.

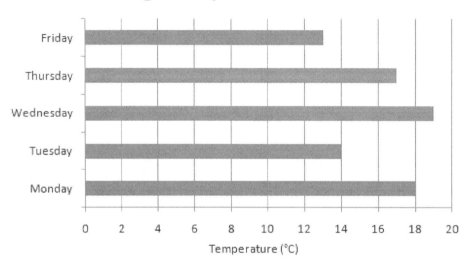

On which day was the high temperature 17°C?

Ⓐ   Tuesday

Ⓑ   Wednesday

Ⓒ   Thursday

Ⓓ   Friday

37 Jordan is putting CDs in a case. She can fit 24 CDs in each row. She has 120 CDs. Which number sentence can be used to find the total number of rows she can fill?

Ⓐ $120 - 24 = \square$

Ⓑ $120 + 24 = \square$

Ⓒ $120 \times 24 = \square$

Ⓓ $120 \div 24 = \square$

38 Which pair of numbers best completes this table?

Number	Number × 10
850	8,500
3,501	35,010
19	190

Ⓐ
28	208

Ⓑ
365	36,500

Ⓒ
1,987	19,870

Ⓓ
6	600

39   Look at the number line below.

Which number does point *S* represent?

Ⓐ   29

Ⓑ   32

Ⓒ   34

Ⓓ   31

40 Allie is buying lunch. The diagram below shows the choices of drinks and meals she has.

Orange Juice		Hamburger
Soda		Hotdog
Apple Juice		Pizza
Water		Salad

How many combinations of 1 drink and 1 meal are possible?

Ⓐ   12

Ⓑ   8

Ⓒ   16

Ⓓ   9

41   The graph below shows the number of pets four girls have.

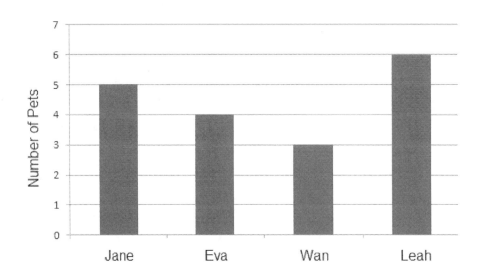

Which two girls have 10 pets in total?

Ⓐ   Jane and Eva

Ⓑ   Wan and Leah

Ⓒ   Eva and Leah

Ⓓ   Leah and Wan

42   It takes Joy from 8 to 12 minutes to walk 1 mile. At this rate, about how long will it take Joy to walk 5 miles?

Ⓐ   90 minutes

Ⓑ   15 minutes

Ⓒ   30 minutes

Ⓓ   50 minutes

END OF TEST

STAAR MATH

GRADE 4

TEST 3

Instructions

The test contains 42 multiple-choice questions. Read each question carefully. Then select the best answer. Fill in the circle for the correct answer.

You can use the mathematic chart on the next page to help you with some of the questions.

MATHEMATICS CHART

You may use this chart to help you answer questions in the test.

LENGTH

Metric
1 meter = 100 centimeters
1 centimeter = 10 millimeters

Customary
1 yard = 3 feet
1 foot = 12 inches

CAPACITY AND VOLUME

Metric
1 liter = 1000 milliliters

Customary
1 gallon = 4 quarts
1 gallon = 128 fluid ounces
1 quart = 2 pints
1 pint = 2 cups
1 cup = 8 fluid ounces

MASS AND WEIGHT

Metric
1 kilogram = 1000 grams
1 gram = 1000 milligrams

Customary
1 ton = 2000 pounds
1 pound = 16 ounces

TIME

Metric
1 year = 365 days
1 year = 12 months
1 year = 52 weeks

Customary
1 week = 7 days
1 day = 24 hours
1 hour = 60 minutes

1   Look at the group of numbers below.

108	86	282
164	190	76

What do these numbers have in common?

Ⓐ   They are all even numbers.

Ⓑ   They are all odd numbers.

Ⓒ   They are all greater than 100.

Ⓓ   They are all less than 200.

2   Bruce has 35 dimes. He puts them in piles of 5. There is the same number of coins in each pile. How could you work out how many piles of coins Bruce would have?

Ⓐ   Divide 35 by 5

Ⓑ   Multiply 5 by 35

Ⓒ   Add 35 and 5

Ⓓ   Subtract 5 from 35

3   Which figure below appears to have exactly two obtuse angles?

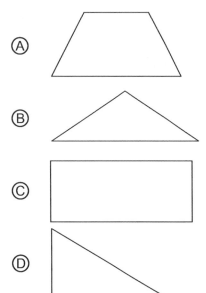

Ⓐ

Ⓑ

Ⓒ

Ⓓ

4   A bakery makes muffins in batches of 12. The bakery made 18 batches of muffins. Which is the best estimate of the number of muffins made?

(A)   100

(B)   400

(C)   250

(D)   200

5   The model below is shaded to show $1\frac{7}{10}$.

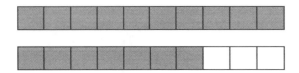

Which decimal does the model represent?

Ⓐ   1.7

Ⓑ   1.07

Ⓒ   0.17

Ⓓ   10.7

6   Which number makes the number sentence below true?

$$18 \div \square = 2$$

Ⓐ   20

Ⓑ   6

Ⓒ   9

Ⓓ   16

7   Which shaded model represents $\frac{5}{4}$?

Ⓐ

Ⓑ

Ⓒ

Ⓓ

8 Which of the following shapes is a pentagon?

Ⓐ

Ⓑ

Ⓒ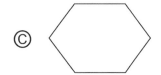

Ⓓ

9 The picture below shows the types of shirts and shorts that Damien has.

How many combinations of 1 shirt and 1 pair of shorts are possible?

Ⓐ 5

Ⓑ 6

Ⓒ 9

Ⓓ 8

10   A school divided its grade 4 students into 6 classes. There were exactly 26 students in each class. How many students were there in all?

Ⓐ   156

Ⓑ   104

Ⓒ   126

Ⓓ   208

11   Which shaded model shows a fraction greater than $\frac{4}{5}$?

Ⓐ

Ⓑ

Ⓒ

Ⓓ

12 A train travels 42 miles in 1 hour. If the train travels at the same speed, which is the best estimate of how long it would take the train to travel 212 miles?

Ⓐ   4 hours

Ⓑ   3 hours

Ⓒ   6 hours

Ⓓ   5 hours

13 Which drawing shows a shape that does **NOT** have a line of symmetry?

Ⓐ

Ⓑ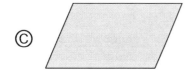

Ⓒ

Ⓓ

14 Mario has $18 to spend on baseball cards. Each packet of baseball cards costs $3. Which of the following shows how to find the number of packets of baseball cards Mario can buy?

Ⓐ   Find the quotient of 18 and 3

Ⓑ   Find the product of 18 and 3

Ⓒ   Find the sum of 18 and 3

Ⓓ   Find the difference between 18 and 3

15 Which is the best estimate of the length of a football?

Ⓐ   10 inches

Ⓑ   10 millimeters

Ⓒ   10 meters

Ⓓ   10 yards

16 Katie saw the sign below at a fruit stand.

If Katie spent $6 on oranges, how many oranges would she get?

Ⓐ   6

Ⓑ   36

Ⓒ   10

Ⓓ   24

17 Which decimal represents the shaded model below?

Ⓐ 0.5

Ⓑ 0.05

Ⓒ 5.0

Ⓓ 5.5

18 Which letter has a line of symmetry?

Ⓐ Z

Ⓑ J

Ⓒ W

Ⓓ R

19   Which fraction does the shaded model below represent?

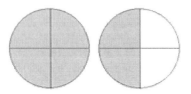

Ⓐ $\dfrac{4}{6}$

Ⓑ $\dfrac{6}{4}$

Ⓒ $\dfrac{2}{4}$

Ⓓ $\dfrac{1}{4}$

20   What is the area of the square shown below?

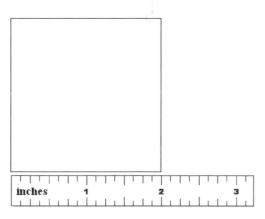

Ⓐ   2 square inches

Ⓑ   4 square inches

Ⓒ   8 square inches

Ⓓ   12 square inches

21 Each number in Set P is related in the same way to the number beside it in Set Q.

Set P	Set Q
2	8
6	12
8	14
10	16

When given a number in Set P, what is one way to find its related number in Set Q?

Ⓐ   Multiply by 4

Ⓑ   Multiply by 2

Ⓒ   Add 6

Ⓓ   Add 8

22 The normal price of a CD player is $298. During a sale, the CD player was $45 less than the normal price. What was the sale price of the CD player?

Ⓐ $343

Ⓑ $333

Ⓒ $263

Ⓓ $253

23 In which number sentence does the number 8 make the equation true?

Ⓐ $48 \div \square = 6$

Ⓑ $\square \div 6 = 48$

Ⓒ $48 \times 6 = \square$

Ⓓ $\square \times 48 = 6$

24 Which figure below does **NOT** have a right angle?

Ⓐ

Ⓑ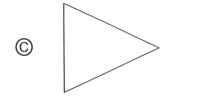

Ⓒ

Ⓓ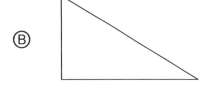

25   Which single transformation is shown below?

Ⓐ   Rotation

Ⓑ   Reflection

Ⓒ   Translation

Ⓓ   Not here

26 Bagels are sold in packets of 4 or packets of 6. Kieran needs to buy exactly 32 bagels. Which set of packets could Kieran buy?

Ⓐ   2 packets of 4 bagels and 4 packets of 6 bagels

Ⓑ   3 packets of 4 bagels and 3 packets of 6 bagels

Ⓒ   4 packets of 4 bagels and 2 packets of 6 bagels

Ⓓ   5 packets of 4 bagels and 1 packet of 6 bagels

27 The graph below shows how long Jason studied for one week.

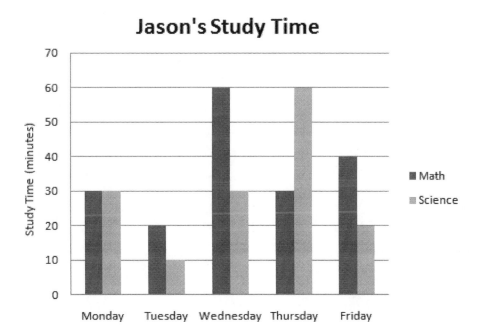

How long did Jason study science for on Thursday?

Ⓐ   30 minutes

Ⓑ   60 minutes

Ⓒ   90 minutes

Ⓓ   20 minutes

28 What is the product of 8 and 9?

    Ⓐ   79

    Ⓑ   81

    Ⓒ   63

    Ⓓ   72

29 Which shape shown has more than 1 line of symmetry?

    Ⓐ

    Ⓑ

    Ⓒ

    Ⓓ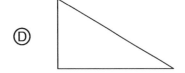

30   Which point on the number line represents 80?

Ⓐ   Point *Q*

Ⓑ   Point *R*

Ⓒ   Point *S*

Ⓓ   Point *T*

31 The table below shows the number of customers a café had on four different days.

Monday	Tuesday	Wednesday	Thursday
487	510	461	469

Which list shows the days in order from least to greatest number of customers?

Ⓐ   Tuesday, Wednesday, Monday, Thursday

Ⓑ   Wednesday, Thursday, Monday, Tuesday

Ⓒ   Wednesday, Monday, Tuesday, Thursday

Ⓓ   Thursday, Monday, Tuesday, Wednesday

32   How many vertices does the shape shown below have?

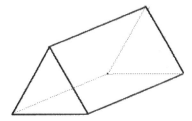

Ⓐ   5

Ⓑ   6

Ⓒ   8

Ⓓ   9

33   A fish tank can hold 20 liters of water. How many milliliters of water can the fish tank hold?

Ⓐ   200 milliliters

Ⓑ   2000 milliliters

Ⓒ   20,000 milliliters

Ⓓ   200,000 milliliters

34   Lee is buying juice. The diagram below shows the flavors and sizes available.

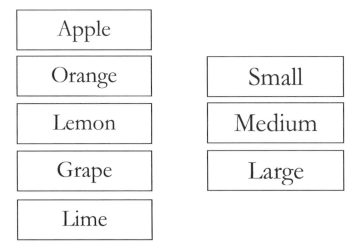

How many combinations of 1 flavor and 1 size are possible?

Ⓐ   8

Ⓑ   15

Ⓒ   24

Ⓓ   25

35   Dean drew these shapes.

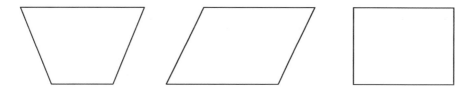

Salma drew these shapes.

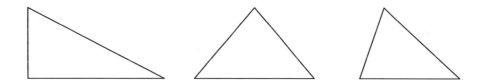

Which shape could be added to Dean's shapes?

Ⓐ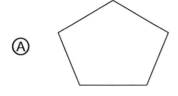

Ⓑ

Ⓒ

Ⓓ

36 Which point on the number line represents 15.8?

Ⓐ   Point *W*

Ⓑ   Point *X*

Ⓒ   Point *Y*

Ⓓ   Point *Z*

37   An array for the number 36 is shown below.

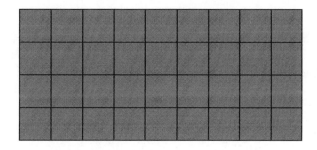

Which number is a factor of 36?

Ⓐ   9

Ⓑ   8

Ⓒ   5

Ⓓ   7

38   Which shape has exactly 5 sides?

Ⓐ   Square

Ⓑ   Hexagon

Ⓒ   Octagon

Ⓓ   Pentagon

39   Which diagram shows a line of symmetry?

Ⓐ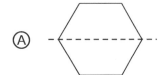

Ⓑ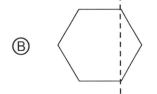

Ⓒ

Ⓓ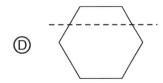

40 Look at the thermometer below.

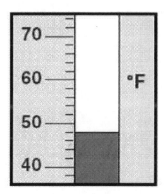

What temperature is shown on the thermometer?

Ⓐ   49°F

Ⓑ   48°F

Ⓒ   45°F

Ⓓ   44°F

41   Which number makes the number sentence below true?

$$\square \div 7 = 9$$

Ⓐ   63

Ⓑ   49

Ⓒ   81

Ⓓ   56

42   Which set of squares has exactly half of the squares shaded?

Ⓐ

Ⓑ

Ⓒ

Ⓓ

END OF TEST

Answer Key

Tracking Student Progress

Use the answer key to score each practice test. After scoring each test, record the score in the Score Tracker at the back of the book.

As the student progresses, test scores will continue to improve as the student develops math skills and gains confidence.

STAAR Objectives and TEKS Expectations

The STAAR test given by the state of Texas tests a specific set of skills and knowledge. The skills and knowledge tested are described in the TEKS Student Expectations, and are divided into 6 broad objectives. These expectations list all the skills and knowledge that students are expected to have.

The answer key identifies the STAAR objective for each question. Use the objectives listed to identify general areas of strength and weakness. Then target revision and instruction accordingly.

The answer key also identifies the specific TEKS expectation that each question is testing. Use the expectations listed to identify skills that the student is lacking. Then target revision and instruction accordingly.

TEST 1 ANSWER KEY

Question	Answer	STAAR Objective	TEKS Expectation
1	B	2: Patterns & Algebra	4.7 A
2	C	6: Processes & Tools	4.14 B
3	B	6: Processes & Tools	4.14 A
4	C	4: Measurement	4.11 B
5	C	4: Measurement	4.12 A
6	D	6: Processes & Tools	4.15 B
7	C	6: Processes & Tools	4.14 C
8	A	4: Measurement	4.11 A
9	A	6: Processes & Tools	4.14 B
10	D	6: Processes & Tools	4.16 A
11	C	5: Probability & Statistics	4.13 A
12	A	6: Processes & Tools	4.16 A
13	C	4: Measurement	4.11 A
14	C	3: Geometry	4.10 A
15	D	3: Geometry	4.9 B
16	B	1: Numbers & Operations	4.5 A
17	C	1: Numbers & Operations	4.4 D
18	D	1: Numbers & Operations	4.5 A
19	C	1: Numbers & Operations	4.4 E
20	B	2: Patterns & Algebra	4.6 B
21	A	1: Numbers & Operations	4.5 B
22	A	3: Geometry	4.8 A
23	D	3: Geometry	4.8 B
24	A	2: Patterns & Algebra	4.6 A
25	B	3: Geometry	4.8 C
26	C	3: Geometry	4.9 B
27	C	3: Geometry	4.9 C
28	B	4: Measurement	4.11 C
29	B	3: Geometry	4.9 C
30	B	4: Measurement	4.11 C
31	C	5: Probability & Statistics	4.13 B
32	C	1: Numbers & Operations	4.4 B
33	C	1: Numbers & Operations	4.3 B
34	D	1: Numbers & Operations	4.1 A
35	B	1: Numbers & Operations	4.2 D
36	A	1: Numbers & Operations	4.1 A
37	B	1: Numbers & Operations	4.4 A
38	A	1: Numbers & Operations	4.3 A
39	D	1: Numbers & Operations	4.3 B
40	C	1: Numbers & Operations	4.4 C
41	B	1: Numbers & Operations	4.4 C
42	A	2: Patterns & Algebra	4.6 B

TEST 2 ANSWER KEY

Question	Answer	STAAR Objective	TEKS Expectation
1	A	1: Numbers & Operations	4.2 C
2	A	1: Numbers & Operations	4.2 D
3	C	1: Numbers & Operations	4.4 A
4	C	2: Patterns & Algebra	4.7 A
5	B	1: Numbers & Operations	4.3 B
6	A	1: Numbers & Operations	4.2 B
7	D	1: Numbers & Operations	4.2 A
8	D	3: Geometry	4.8 A
9	B	3: Geometry	4.9 C
10	D	1: Numbers & Operations	4.1 A
11	C	1: Numbers & Operations	4.1 B
12	B	1: Numbers & Operations	4.1 A
13	A	1: Numbers & Operations	4.2 C
14	D	1: Numbers & Operations	4.4 C
15	C	1: Numbers & Operations	4.4 C
16	C	1: Numbers & Operations	4.4 E
17	C	1: Numbers & Operations	4.5 A
18	A	1: Numbers & Operations	4.3 A
19	D	1: Numbers & Operations	4.3 A
20	D	3: Geometry	4.8 C
21	D	3: Geometry	4.8 B
22	B	4: Measurement	4.11 B
23	D	4: Measurement	4.11 C
24	B	4: Measurement	4.12 A
25	C	6: Processes & Tools	4.14 C
26	D	6: Processes & Tools	4.15 B
27	C	1: Numbers & Operations	4.4 A
28	D	3: Geometry	4.8 A
29	B	3: Geometry	4.8 B
30	D	6: Processes & Tools	4.14 A
31	D	6: Processes & Tools	4.16 A
32	B	2: Patterns & Algebra	4.6 A
33	C	3: Geometry	4.9 B
34	D	1: Numbers & Operations	4.2 A
35	A	3: Geometry	4.9 B
36	C	5: Probability & Statistics	4.13 B
37	D	1: Numbers & Operations	4.4 B
38	C	2: Patterns & Algebra	4.6 B
39	B	3: Geometry	4.10 A
40	C	5: Probability & Statistics	4.13 A
41	C	5: Probability & Statistics	4.13 B
42	D	6: Processes & Tools	4.14 B

TEST 3 ANSWER KEY

Question	Answer	STAAR Objective	TEKS Expectation
1	A	6: Processes & Tools	4.16 A
2	A	1: Numbers & Operations	4.4 B
3	A	3: Geometry	4.8 A
4	D	1: Numbers & Operations	4.5 B
5	A	1: Numbers & Operations	4.2 D
6	C	2: Patterns & Algebra	4.6 A
7	C	1: Numbers & Operations	4.2 B
8	A	3: Geometry	4.8 C
9	B	5: Probability & Statistics	4.13 A
10	A	1: Numbers & Operations	4.4 D
11	D	1: Numbers & Operations	4.2 C
12	D	1: Numbers & Operations	4.5 B
13	C	3: Geometry	4.9 C
14	A	6: Processes & Tools	4.15 B
15	A	4: Measurement	4.11 A
16	D	1: Numbers & Operations	4.4 D
17	A	1: Numbers & Operations	4.1 B
18	C	3: Geometry	4.9 C
19	B	1: Numbers & Operations	4.2 B
20	C	4: Measurement	4.11 A
21	C	2: Patterns & Algebra	4.7 A
22	D	1: Numbers & Operations	4.3 A
23	A	2: Patterns & Algebra	4.6 A
24	C	3: Geometry	4.8 A
25	C	3: Geometry	4.9 B
26	A	6: Processes & Tools	4.14 B
27	B	5: Probability & Statistics	4.13 B
28	D	1: Numbers & Operations	4.4 C
29	C	3: Geometry	4.9 C
30	B	3: Geometry	4.10 A
31	B	1: Numbers & Operations	4.1 A
32	B	3: Geometry	4.8 C
33	C	4: Measurement	4.11 B
34	B	5: Probability & Statistics	4.13 A
35	B	6: Processes & Tools	4.16 A
36	B	3: Geometry	4.10 A
37	A	1: Numbers & Operations	4.4 A
38	D	3: Geometry	4.8 C
39	A	3: Geometry	4.9 C
40	B	4: Measurement	4.12 A
41	A	2: Patterns & Algebra	4.6 A
42	A	1: Numbers & Operations	4.2 C

STAAR MATH STATE STANDARDS
Grade 4 Objectives and Student Expectations

Objective 1: Numbers, Operations, and Quantitative Reasoning	
4.1 A	The student is expected to use place value to read, write, compare, and order whole numbers through 999,999,999.
4.1 B	The student is expected to use place value to read, write, compare, and order decimals involving tenths and hundredths, including money, using pictorial models.
4.2 A	The student is expected to use pictorial models to generate equivalent fractions.
4.2 B	The student is expected to model fraction quantities greater than one using pictorial models.
4.2 C	The student is expected to compare and order fractions using pictorial models.
4.2 D	The student is expected to relate decimals to fractions that name tenths and hundredths using pictorial models.
4.3 A	The student is expected to use addition and subtraction to solve problems involving whole numbers.
4.3 B	The student is expected to add and subtract decimals to the hundredths place using pictorial models.
4.4 A	The student is expected to model factors and products using arrays and area models.
4.4 B	The student is expected to represent multiplication and division situations in picture, word, and number form.
4.4 C	The student is expected to recall and apply multiplication facts through 12×12.
4.4 D	The student is expected to use multiplication to solve problems (no more than two digits times two digits without technology).
4.4 E	The student is expected to use division to solve problems (no more than one-digit divisors and three-digit dividends without technology).

4.5 A	The student is expected to round whole numbers to the nearest ten, hundred, or thousand to approximate reasonable results in problem situations.
4.5 B	The student is expected to use strategies including rounding and compatible numbers to estimate solutions to multiplication and division problems.

Objective 2: Patterns, Relationships, and Algebraic Thinking	
4.6 A	The student is expected to use patterns and relationships to develop strategies to remember basic multiplication and division facts.
4.6 B	The student is expected to use patterns to multiply by 10 and 100.
4.7 A	The student is expected to describe the relationship between two sets of related data such as ordered pairs in a table.

Objective 3: Geometry and Spatial Reasoning	
4.8 A	The student is expected to identify and describe right, acute, and obtuse angles.
4.8 B	The student is expected to identify and describe parallel and intersecting (including perpendicular) lines using pictorial models.
4.8 C	The student is expected to use essential attributes to define two- and three-dimensional geometric figures.
4.9 B	The student is expected to use translations, reflections, and rotations to verify that two shapes are congruent.
4.9 C	The student is expected to use reflections to verify that a shape has symmetry.
4.10 A	The student is expected to locate and name points on a number line using whole numbers, fractions such as halves and fourths, and decimals such as tenths.

Objective 4: Measurement	
4.11 A	The student is expected to estimate and use measurement tools to determine length (including perimeter), area, capacity, and weight/mass using standard units SI (metric) and customary.
4.11 B	The student is expected to perform simple conversions between different units of length, between different units of capacity, and between different units of weight within the customary measurement system.
4.11 C	The student is expected to use models of standard cubic units to measure volume.
4.12 A	The student is expected to use a thermometer to measure temperature and changes in temperature.

Objective 5: Probability and Statistics	
4.13 A	The student is expected to use pictures to make generalizations about determining all possible combinations of a given set of data or of objects in a problem situation.
4.13 B	The student is expected to interpret bar graphs.

Objective 6: Underlying Processes and Mathematical Tools	
4.14 A	The student is expected to identify the mathematics in everyday situations.
4.14 B	The student is expected to solve problems that incorporate understanding the problem, making a plan, carrying out the plan, and evaluating the solution for reasonableness.
4.14 C	The student is expected to select or develop an appropriate problem-solving plan or strategy, including drawing a picture, looking for a pattern, systematic guessing and checking, acting it out, making a table, working a simpler problem, or working backwards to solve a problem.
4.15 B	The student is expected to relate informal language to mathematical language and symbols.
4.16 A	The student is expected to make generalizations from patterns or sets of examples and nonexamples.

MULTIPLE CHOICE ANSWER SHEET

TEST 1

1	Ⓐ Ⓑ Ⓒ Ⓓ	16	Ⓐ Ⓑ Ⓒ Ⓓ	31	Ⓐ Ⓑ Ⓒ Ⓓ
2	Ⓐ Ⓑ Ⓒ Ⓓ	17	Ⓐ Ⓑ Ⓒ Ⓓ	32	Ⓐ Ⓑ Ⓒ Ⓓ
3	Ⓐ Ⓑ Ⓒ Ⓓ	18	Ⓐ Ⓑ Ⓒ Ⓓ	33	Ⓐ Ⓑ Ⓒ Ⓓ
4	Ⓐ Ⓑ Ⓒ Ⓓ	19	Ⓐ Ⓑ Ⓒ Ⓓ	34	Ⓐ Ⓑ Ⓒ Ⓓ
5	Ⓐ Ⓑ Ⓒ Ⓓ	20	Ⓐ Ⓑ Ⓒ Ⓓ	35	Ⓐ Ⓑ Ⓒ Ⓓ
6	Ⓐ Ⓑ Ⓒ Ⓓ	21	Ⓐ Ⓑ Ⓒ Ⓓ	36	Ⓐ Ⓑ Ⓒ Ⓓ
7	Ⓐ Ⓑ Ⓒ Ⓓ	22	Ⓐ Ⓑ Ⓒ Ⓓ	37	Ⓐ Ⓑ Ⓒ Ⓓ
8	Ⓐ Ⓑ Ⓒ Ⓓ	23	Ⓐ Ⓑ Ⓒ Ⓓ	38	Ⓐ Ⓑ Ⓒ Ⓓ
9	Ⓐ Ⓑ Ⓒ Ⓓ	24	Ⓐ Ⓑ Ⓒ Ⓓ	39	Ⓐ Ⓑ Ⓒ Ⓓ
10	Ⓐ Ⓑ Ⓒ Ⓓ	25	Ⓐ Ⓑ Ⓒ Ⓓ	40	Ⓐ Ⓑ Ⓒ Ⓓ
11	Ⓐ Ⓑ Ⓒ Ⓓ	26	Ⓐ Ⓑ Ⓒ Ⓓ	41	Ⓐ Ⓑ Ⓒ Ⓓ
12	Ⓐ Ⓑ Ⓒ Ⓓ	27	Ⓐ Ⓑ Ⓒ Ⓓ	42	Ⓐ Ⓑ Ⓒ Ⓓ
13	Ⓐ Ⓑ Ⓒ Ⓓ	28	Ⓐ Ⓑ Ⓒ Ⓓ		
14	Ⓐ Ⓑ Ⓒ Ⓓ	29	Ⓐ Ⓑ Ⓒ Ⓓ		
15	Ⓐ Ⓑ Ⓒ Ⓓ	30	Ⓐ Ⓑ Ⓒ Ⓓ		

MULTIPLE CHOICE ANSWER SHEET

TEST 2

1	Ⓐ Ⓑ Ⓒ Ⓓ	16	Ⓐ Ⓑ Ⓒ Ⓓ	31	Ⓐ Ⓑ Ⓒ Ⓓ
2	Ⓐ Ⓑ Ⓒ Ⓓ	17	Ⓐ Ⓑ Ⓒ Ⓓ	32	Ⓐ Ⓑ Ⓒ Ⓓ
3	Ⓐ Ⓑ Ⓒ Ⓓ	18	Ⓐ Ⓑ Ⓒ Ⓓ	33	Ⓐ Ⓑ Ⓒ Ⓓ
4	Ⓐ Ⓑ Ⓒ Ⓓ	19	Ⓐ Ⓑ Ⓒ Ⓓ	34	Ⓐ Ⓑ Ⓒ Ⓓ
5	Ⓐ Ⓑ Ⓒ Ⓓ	20	Ⓐ Ⓑ Ⓒ Ⓓ	35	Ⓐ Ⓑ Ⓒ Ⓓ
6	Ⓐ Ⓑ Ⓒ Ⓓ	21	Ⓐ Ⓑ Ⓒ Ⓓ	36	Ⓐ Ⓑ Ⓒ Ⓓ
7	Ⓐ Ⓑ Ⓒ Ⓓ	22	Ⓐ Ⓑ Ⓒ Ⓓ	37	Ⓐ Ⓑ Ⓒ Ⓓ
8	Ⓐ Ⓑ Ⓒ Ⓓ	23	Ⓐ Ⓑ Ⓒ Ⓓ	38	Ⓐ Ⓑ Ⓒ Ⓓ
9	Ⓐ Ⓑ Ⓒ Ⓓ	24	Ⓐ Ⓑ Ⓒ Ⓓ	39	Ⓐ Ⓑ Ⓒ Ⓓ
10	Ⓐ Ⓑ Ⓒ Ⓓ	25	Ⓐ Ⓑ Ⓒ Ⓓ	40	Ⓐ Ⓑ Ⓒ Ⓓ
11	Ⓐ Ⓑ Ⓒ Ⓓ	26	Ⓐ Ⓑ Ⓒ Ⓓ	41	Ⓐ Ⓑ Ⓒ Ⓓ
12	Ⓐ Ⓑ Ⓒ Ⓓ	27	Ⓐ Ⓑ Ⓒ Ⓓ	42	Ⓐ Ⓑ Ⓒ Ⓓ
13	Ⓐ Ⓑ Ⓒ Ⓓ	28	Ⓐ Ⓑ Ⓒ Ⓓ		
14	Ⓐ Ⓑ Ⓒ Ⓓ	29	Ⓐ Ⓑ Ⓒ Ⓓ		
15	Ⓐ Ⓑ Ⓒ Ⓓ	30	Ⓐ Ⓑ Ⓒ Ⓓ		

MULTIPLE CHOICE ANSWER SHEET

TEST 3

1 Ⓐ Ⓑ Ⓒ Ⓓ	16 Ⓐ Ⓑ Ⓒ Ⓓ	31 Ⓐ Ⓑ Ⓒ Ⓓ
2 Ⓐ Ⓑ Ⓒ Ⓓ	17 Ⓐ Ⓑ Ⓒ Ⓓ	32 Ⓐ Ⓑ Ⓒ Ⓓ
3 Ⓐ Ⓑ Ⓒ Ⓓ	18 Ⓐ Ⓑ Ⓒ Ⓓ	33 Ⓐ Ⓑ Ⓒ Ⓓ
4 Ⓐ Ⓑ Ⓒ Ⓓ	19 Ⓐ Ⓑ Ⓒ Ⓓ	34 Ⓐ Ⓑ Ⓒ Ⓓ
5 Ⓐ Ⓑ Ⓒ Ⓓ	20 Ⓐ Ⓑ Ⓒ Ⓓ	35 Ⓐ Ⓑ Ⓒ Ⓓ
6 Ⓐ Ⓑ Ⓒ Ⓓ	21 Ⓐ Ⓑ Ⓒ Ⓓ	36 Ⓐ Ⓑ Ⓒ Ⓓ
7 Ⓐ Ⓑ Ⓒ Ⓓ	22 Ⓐ Ⓑ Ⓒ Ⓓ	37 Ⓐ Ⓑ Ⓒ Ⓓ
8 Ⓐ Ⓑ Ⓒ Ⓓ	23 Ⓐ Ⓑ Ⓒ Ⓓ	38 Ⓐ Ⓑ Ⓒ Ⓓ
9 Ⓐ Ⓑ Ⓒ Ⓓ	24 Ⓐ Ⓑ Ⓒ Ⓓ	39 Ⓐ Ⓑ Ⓒ Ⓓ
10 Ⓐ Ⓑ Ⓒ Ⓓ	25 Ⓐ Ⓑ Ⓒ Ⓓ	40 Ⓐ Ⓑ Ⓒ Ⓓ
11 Ⓐ Ⓑ Ⓒ Ⓓ	26 Ⓐ Ⓑ Ⓒ Ⓓ	41 Ⓐ Ⓑ Ⓒ Ⓓ
12 Ⓐ Ⓑ Ⓒ Ⓓ	27 Ⓐ Ⓑ Ⓒ Ⓓ	42 Ⓐ Ⓑ Ⓒ Ⓓ
13 Ⓐ Ⓑ Ⓒ Ⓓ	28 Ⓐ Ⓑ Ⓒ Ⓓ	
14 Ⓐ Ⓑ Ⓒ Ⓓ	29 Ⓐ Ⓑ Ⓒ Ⓓ	
15 Ⓐ Ⓑ Ⓒ Ⓓ	30 Ⓐ Ⓑ Ⓒ Ⓓ	

Score Tracker

	Score
Test 1	**/42**
Test 2	**/42**
Test 3	**/42**

TEXAS TEST PREP STUDENT QUIZ BOOK

For additional math test prep, get the Texas Test Prep Student Quiz Book. It contains one quiz for every skill tested on the Texas state tests. It can be used in combination with this Practice Test Book for focused revision to target gaps in knowledge and address student weaknesses.

After revision using the quiz book, take another practice test and see the improvement!

TEXAS TEST PREP READING

Help with the Texas STAAR tests is also available for reading!

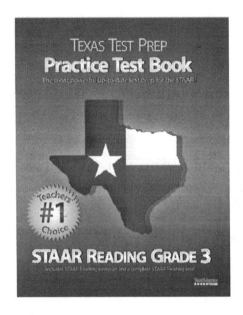

- Practice Test Book and Reading Workbook available
- Covers every reading skill needed by Texas students
- Books available from Grades 3 through to 8

TEXAS TEST PREP MATH
Check out the full range of math books available!

 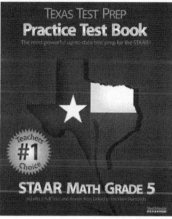 

- Practice Test Book and Student Quiz Book available
- Covers every math skill needed by Texas students
- Books available from Grades 3 through to 8

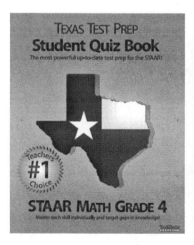 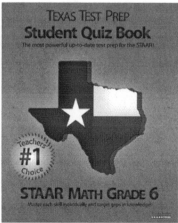 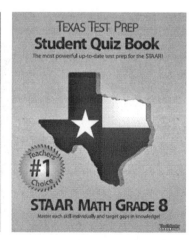